1

## Re-Claiming Reality

Growing up in this world we develop ways to deal with its
madness. It's a struggle, and the explanations we get
contradict the deep knowledge we brought with us. This
knowledge is a string that can never be broken. Every now and
then we feel it vibrate when good things happen. It might be a
wonderful love, something too big for comprehension yet true
beyond doubt. We know truth like fish may know water, alive in
it without thinking about it. As humans, we use thoughts, but
thoughts need words. Words enable us to build fake realities,
otherwise nobody would seriously believe that violence could
ever solve a problem. As years go by, however, we see the
pattern: We are chased against each other by the mechanics in
our brain. Even the worst enemies are members of the same
club: the brotherhood of brain slaves.


We are used to acting on what we THINK is real. To break free
we must access what lies beyond the walls of logical thinking.
Let us re-claim our deep knowledge of life. There is no direct
access but we can prepare by withdrawing our attention from
fake realities. When we take responsibility for our inner space,
we put an end to the dominance of our brain mechanism.
Instead of letting it control our lives we can use our brain as
the great service instrument it is. A brain needs guidance, it
cannot guide us. In fact, thoughts cannot follow us through the
door which we are about to open here and now.

## This is why we came here:

We are stargates for the flow of life into the manifest dimension on earth.
It is our destiny to translate unspeakable knowledge into songs, make our
hands build roads through the night, and travel on good dreams.

<br>

**This is how we lost the way:**

On brain highway, we keep replacing reality with second-hand constructions - ideas, words, memories - and their accompanying emotions on the physical level. Unawares of this fact we have established a roaring, stampeding illusion. Let´s press the reset button.

Quit the wall game.

Start taking responsibility
for your inner space.

# CONTENTS

# 1. WHO ARE YOU?

**STEP ONE:** Imagine that everything you know, everything you are is stored in that suitcase. You carry it with you all the time. It is your personality. Don´t just look at the picture: IMAGINE this! NOW!

You are like nobody else. No matter how you feel about yourself, in the entire universe there has never been anybody exactly like you, and there will never ever be. You are a unique mixture of ingredients: You came with some, others were kicked in, some you picked up along the way. You have your strengths and weaknesses, your memories, your plans, your favourite movies, your doubts and fears, things you love and things you hate.

**STEP TWO**: Take a look at your own unique personality. Identify three of your character traits. Be honest. Grab a pen and write them into the lid of your personality case. STOP! Grab that pen. Do it NOW!

Your personality works for you as a compass and a map, all in one. It is a habit you share with most people. We grow up believing that reality and the contents of our brain are one and the same thing.

**STEP THREE**: Where do you keep your personality?

**STEP FOUR**: There is no other place for your personality but your brain.
Even if you think it´s in your left foot this is a thought, and thoughts
inhabit your brain. Now don´t worry about forgetting one or the other
ingredient of your personality, and it doesn´t matter if you call some
subconscious and others by different names. Simply see that this case in
your brain contains ALL of them. Take a moment to really GRASP this.

11

**STEP FIVE**: Now look at the personality bundle in your head and answer this question: If this bundle you´re looking at is you –

## Who is looking at it here and now?

You cannot sit inside a house and look at it from the street at the same time. When you look at the unique bundle that you are, you are definitely looking from some other place, right? What is that other place?

It´s your AWARENESS. Awareness is not inside your bundle. It is your link with life, with everything. Awareness lets YOU look from a real but neglected inner space that has always been there.

## 2. WHAT IS AWARENESS?

Looking at your personality case makes you aware that there is a neglected sphere that you can enter. This awareness may last only for a short moment at first. Immediately afterwards your brain mechanism rejects that sphere as useless nonsense. When its dominance is threatened, your brain acts like a sea mine ready to destroy the enemy vessel - even if this means suicide. Awareness threatens our familiar definition of who we think we are. In this definition the very existence of a wideopen space outside of brain control seems revolting. Brain logics always imagine a conflict between

1. The #1YOU who you really are

2. the #2you who you THINK you are

**The purpose** of this book is to make you aware of the limits of #2you and the infinite reality of #1YOU. Break the dominance of brain mechanics, overcome doubts and fears, and dive into real life.

**The reason** for this effort is that #2you darkens your life, splits up mankind into hostile groups, and destroys the ecosphere, while #1YOU is the ticket out of this mess. Watch the news: Without guidance by #1YOU veal oil beef hugged.

**The obstacle** along the road is our tradition of treating #2you as real, and #1YOU as fiction.


Once you see who you **really** are the illusion of a **conflict** with who you **think** you are is dissolved.

# Now develop your awareness:

Awareness happens when our brain mechanism does not interfere. Since we grew up in a culture that takes brain constructions for real, though, that mechanism interferes all the time. When we talk about awareness, our brain immediately starts building roads to what it imagines awareness might be. It is programmed that way: Identify a goal, develop a strategy, go and get it. If awareness could be achieved that way it would of course remain inside the brain. The challenge is: Discovering our #1YOU without a memory of how we did it. #1YOU is alive and real, but any description of it is a snapshot of nothing. Awareness happens only here and now. You cannot spit in the air a second ago, and you can´t spit a second after now. When you spit, it´s always at this very moment. Brain mechanics keep asking: How can I develop awareness? It is – again and again - the wrong question. There is no road from here to there. Neither guru nor method, no road or teacher can take you beyond but what you can do is: Take responsibility for your inner space. Slow down your train of thoughts. Awareness may happen now or never, but even while you prepare yourself you will feel more alive than before. Some people find that riding a mountain bike in a beautiful countryside helps them stop their brain train, others might get the same result by taking care of the flowers in their garden - but they rarely see the importance of that state of ´no mind´.

# You are now leaving

the sector of administrative brain control.

### 3. Take Responsibility for Your Inner Space

Imagine that all people on earth live in different rooms of the same old house. You grew up in one of these rooms, believing that the wallpaper shows the real world. Your intuition lets you see confusing things through a window sometimes but a second afterwards your brain calls these visions a dream to feel safe again. Awareness – in contrast - means opening your personality case, looking at the contents, letting go of what you don´t need, leaving your room, and walking out the front door.

Beyond the doorstep is a sphere where our brain cannot follow.

**Here comes a short guide from your room to the front door:**

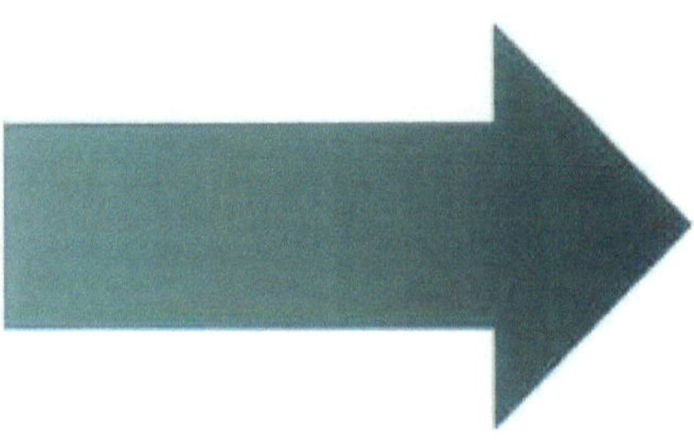

## Two sides of the same coin

Feelings are the physical symptoms of thoughts. Watch a film and identify with a protagonist that appeals to you. Many films evoke strong feelings. Your body will react to what happens to the character you identify with. Then withdraw your attention, as hard as it seems, and you will withdraw the power this character has over your feelings. In real life, every thought you identify with controls you. You give it this power. Criminal politicians use this mechanism to control you, and their most effective instruments are thoughts that generate fear and hatred. If you believe that you must defend yourself and your loved ones, and if somebody then promises he can solve the problem by using violence, even madness sounds logical. Killing for love, starting a war to save peace seems to make sense in a mad context. And how about music? If you like a tune it will transport the meaning of the lyrics much better than just reading them. Still: Feelings are no compass. Never. Logic is no better. Thoughts and feelings are two sides of the same false coin that doesn't buy you the good life you want.


## How can I be myself?

Well, here we come back to our personality bundle: WHO do you think is asking this question? Get it? Your brain bundle is trying the impossible again - reaching into the reality beyond. Your brain may generate thoughts like: One day, if I read this book and do some exercises, I will find myself and all problems will disappear. What your brain mechanism is looking for is a result it can reach and hold onto - a set of vowels and consonants that make up words, the stuff thoughts are made of. Try as long as you will but words are not real things. So do not try to grasp your "true self". You need not and you cannot tear down any walls when these walls are illusions created by words – because there ARE no walls. Don't waste your time on Brain Road.

## Forget about happiness

No matter what you seek for yourself – it strengthens your belief that you don´t have it and deepens the conflict. You cannot strive for happiness. Your brain believes in deficits or assets alike as if they were real. Look at your suffering, your longing for change, your envy, your theories on who is to blame – these brain constructions are products of your brain mechanics. Be aware of how brain mechanics make you worry more than necessary, thus blocking the energy you could use to drag yourself out of the swamp. Awareness is the magnet for success. Therefore, never say: I am unhappy. Say instead: Something in me is unhappy. Conflicts always arise between simple realities and your ideas of what should be different. You will find that any situation is simply as it is. It´s your thoughts which make it into a problem. Calm down your thoughts. Wait and put them to work after some input from beyond.

## Enter the present moment

Feel the pulse in your fingertips. Be aware of the thoughts that wander through your mind and let them pass. See how you like some thoughts and how you reject others. See how thoughts evoke feelings, physical reactions. Will this exercise get you closer to enlightenment? NO, because this is nothing you can achieve by any technique. When you think you have it it´s gone for sure. Why then practice at all? You know the answer.

## Eternity is now

When you think about life you are going down brain road. It cannot be otherwise because thoughts are the only figments your brain can handle. All thoughts either come when the moment is gone, or they expect a moment that has not yet happened. Therefore, life is this very moment, as you are reading this. Since there is nothing else but this moment, this moment and eternity are no different. If you think otherwise you are dealing with constructions.

## What´s missing?

Stop reading now and ask yourself: What´s missing in my life
<u>right now</u>? This forces you to realize what´s going on at this
very moment. Your brain will approach an overload. Watch your
thoughts get sucked into the usual swamp. The moment you
realize you are NOT here now is the exact moment when you
are here. This is awareness. No big deal really, but it changes
everything.

**Don´t act just because you have a good reason.**

When you talk to somebody, you talk as the personality bundle
you think you are, and you have an image of the person you
are talking to. The other person does the same. Look:

1. You are not your personality bundle

2. The other person is not his/her personality bundle

3. Your assumptions are not the other person.

4. The other person´s assumptions of you are not you.

Most relationships are new or old mixtures of these four
ingredients. You can think about this simple truth but you
might as well go fishing. You cannot change things by any plan
you come up with. Fortunately, however, since you cannot
consciously make that change, there is nothing you NEED to do
either - except being aware of the reality that happens here
and now. At first glance, admittedly, this reality is probably not
as colorful as you wish. Stay aware by all means anyway. The
fog will rise, the road will reveal itself.


**Friends or just inmates of the same brain ghetto?**

In a situation where everybody else expresses strong opinions,
do not join in their game. Say that you are not sure things are
quite that easy without giving reasons. You may shrink in the
others´s esteem. Watch inside if you feel hurt and want to
regain respect. Feel the strong sucking of the others´
expectations but do not satisfy them. Stay aware of the space
you are creating by not acting as a brain slave. Pay the price of
isolation for a little while. It is lower than you fear. Why should
you do this? Well, for one thing it makes you realize how fragile
your relationships are. Most are based on similar perceptions of
how things are and how they should be otherwise. You can´t
swim in a pool of illusions, but you can´t drown either.

### Oh, those idiots

If others behave in ways that you find unacceptable,
understand that in their heads the same brain mechanism is at
work as in your own - just the contents are different. Do not
take their behaviour personal because they just act as puppets
on strings. Be aware of this. Do not judge them. That doesn´t
mean you must tolerate physical abuse but do not make
yourself a slave of your brain mechanism by falling into the trap
of retaliation. Break the circle of violence.


### Watch the inner ocean.

Your personal history is an inner ocean, and you are sailing on
it with dragons and unicorns. Do not mingle in their quarrels,
do not analyze. See your uncertainty in this vast space but
search no island. You are not lost. The horizon is a thought and
behind it is just another thought. Don´t be afraid. If you let go
you will not drown. Flap the wings of awareness. Watch your
brain mechanism drag you down as it finds logical arguments.
Watch how it makes resistance feel like heroism, how it figures
out a route to treasure island. Your brain mechanism is
extremely creative when it comes to retaining its dominance.
Don´t be afraid to dive into its colorful illusions but rise again,
come back out, see the light reflecting on the waves of your
ocean. Storms must end, clouds will pass, stay aware.


### Us and them: Phony manipulation

Watch yourself adapt your behaviour to get what you want.
Does your voice on the phone sound different? Why? What
would you like the other person to think? Do not be satisfied
with easy answers.

**The river flows to the sea.**

When something you don´t like is happening here and now, it is completely crazy to resist, because it is already there. Your impulse to resist comes because your brain bundle rejects phenomena that differ from the images it has constructed. In real life, YOU are not a figment of your brain. Nobody is attacking you, so do not defend yourself if there´s no physical abuse. Don´t listen to your brain rebellion - it´s similar to not scratching an itch. When your brain bundle identifies a conflict stay on top of the situation. Do not react. Resistance supports your bundle´s preposterous claim that it is really YOU.


**Trees don´t catch the wind.**

All things must pass. Watch how your personality bundle constantly tries to drag your living moments down into its storage for past or future illusions. See how addicted you are to that practice. See how it governs your life, chasing you from one kingdom to the next in endless battles. See how any new way to look at things is translated as "complicated" by your old ego that fears changes. Stay aware and experience how awareness dissolves these brain games. You win this race when you give it up.

**What am I going to think of next?**

Ask yourself this question. It will stop your train of thoughts for a while and make you aware. You won´t think, won´t hope, won´t remember, and if you do, you will be aware of it.


**Approach silence**

You do not need to sit on a nail board or meditate on a mountainside to be aware. Since you live in the middle of this wonderfully connected universe you can access inner silence everywhere at any time. So rock around the clock: Practice awareness with simple exercises, e.g. look at any object that is not man made, a tree, a flower on your table. This will make you aware of your brain train´s noise. You cannot consciously stop that train. Awareness means realizing the noise and your futile efforts to stop it. Now realize the difference between awareness and silence: Silence is the station you can wake up in without knowing how you got there, or in other words: You get there when you quit trying. Awareness prepares you – it´s not a method to gain silence, since silence is a state of no-mind beyond thought.

Another exercise is when you simply focus on your body, e.g. where and how your body touches the chair you´re sitting on. Innumerable exercises can slow down your brain train. They won´t take you across the border into silence but every time you are observing, listening to the voices and pictures of your inner space, even if it´s just for a minute, you are becoming more aware of the boring, repetitive efforts of your thought mechanism to retain its dominant position. Be assured: You need not stop trains or break through walls because these things are illusions on this side of the fence, if fact – they ARE the fence.

## The illusion of time.

Time is taking the bite out of everything, constantly changing what used to be. Time seems a thief, stealing your life in bits and pieces, and it seems that you are its helpless victim. When do you feel time? When looking in the mirror? Nevermind the gold mines of anti-aging popes. Here we are focussing on the mental illusion of time, not the seasonal changes in nature.

You feel time strongest when you resist what is happening at this moment, when you have planned a different future and the road you have chosen doesn´t take you there. You feel time as a conflict when circumstances block you. Watch your tension while driving in heavy traffic. The slow driver in front of you causes what the Buddhists call ´suffering´. Your thought mechanism creates this conflict all the time.

We are alive in the middle of a greater reality, but our brain reduces life to a bunch of sticks and stones and figures and facts because it needs the illusion of control. Again, we are talking about time as a mental illusion. Real time just means wrinkles in your face and snow on the fields. There is no conflict. Conflicts are staged by United Brainworks, that crazy theatre company. Go into Globe Theatre, be aware of the action on stage, and discover the whole show as a gate into reality. Then exit the theatre and stage your own show when you´re ready.

## Epilogue

For a long time this world has been going round and round in madness mode. Ignorant of their own limitations, our brain mechanics have led us down dead-end streets with fancy names. Still, all of us are equals insofar as no brain has access to direct knowledge. How we deal with that fact is every newcomer´s lifelong task. While every culture knows men and women who sense our connectedness beyond what their brain defines as real, most people deny what they cannot put their hands on. These people settle down for explanations. As different explanations meet in our globalized world, however, the result is not simply a colorful variety of fairy tales. It means an overload of realities, and this overload seems to take away the floor from under people´s feet. They do not see the waning of their familiar explanations as an emerging opportunity to tear down walls. They reject the truth about the king´s clothes. In their world, their brain ID is king. When he is threatened, their whole existence seems at stake. The consequences are fear and hatred.

Brain mechanics separate and chase us against each other. We agree to be victims when we allow brain logics to govern our actions. Instead of uniting our energies in the healing of our awareness-problem we waste our resources and follow worthless brain slaves into disaster.

Once we realize our brain-handicap we can tackle the resulting problems directly. No outside enemy or natural blockade can be blamed for reproducing the present misery. If we want it, nothing can stop our awareness from growing. We work and breathe and suffer and love in the middle of a mystery. We need not explain – just live in it together. We have always been more than we think.

**THE BEGINNING**